Natural Environment Research Council

Institute of Terrestrial Ecology

Butterfly Research in I.T.E.

Marney L. Hall
Institute of Terrestrial Ecology
Monks Wood Experimental Station
Huntingdon

2

Printed in Great Britain by
The Cambrian News,
Aberystwyth.

Published in 1981 by
Institute of Terrestrial Ecology
68 Hills Road
Cambridge
CB2 1LA
0223 (Cambridge) 69745

ISBN 0 904282 46 5

The cover shows the life-cycle and habitat of the white admiral
butterfly. All photographs by E. Pollard, except of the adult female
which is by M. S. Warren.
Clockwise from the top: Marks Wood National Nature Reserve,
habitat; adult female; egg; hibernaculum; fifth instar larva; pupa.

ACKNOWLEDGEMENT
The author would like to thank Dr. J. P. Dempster and Dr. E. Pollard
for their help in the preparation of the manuscript. I also wish to
thank Dr. Pollard, Mr. Martin Warren, Dr. J. A. Thomas and Mr. J.
Heath for the loan of their many colour slides. Finally I wish to thank
Mrs. D. Plant for typing the manuscript.

The Institute of Terrestrial Ecology (ITE) was established in 1973
from the former Nature Conservancy's research stations and staff,
joined later by the Institute of Tree Biology and the Culture Centres
of Algae and Protozoa. ITE contributes to and draws upon the
collective knowledge of the fourteen sister institutes which make up
the *Natural Environment Research Council,* spanning all the
environmental sciences.

The Institute studies the factors determining the structure,
composition and processes of land and freshwater systems, and of
individual plant and animal species. It is developing a sounder
scientific basis for predicting and modelling environmental trends
arising from natural or man-made change. The results of this
research are available to those responsible for the protection,
management and wise use of our natural resources.

Nearly half of ITE's work is research commissioned by customers,
such as the Nature Conservancy Council who require information for
wildlife conservation, the Department of Energy, the Department of
the Environment and the EEC.
The remainder is fundamental research supported by NERC.

ITE's expertise is widely used by international organisations in
overseas projects and programmes of research.

Mrs. Marney Hall
Institute of Terrestrial Ecology
Monks Wood Experimental Station
Abbots Ripton
Huntington
Cambridgeshire
PE17 2LS
04873 (Abbots Ripton)381

Contents

Introduction

There are fifty-eight species of butterfly which regularly breed in Britain today. Several are extremely common, in some cases pests, such as the small white *Pieris rapae* (Plate 1). Others arrive each year from the continent to breed, but rarely survive the winter here, whilst others again have adapted themselves both to our climate and to the surprising wealth of habitats such a small country as Great Britain has to offer.

Very little, if any, of lowland Britain has survived man's influence unchanged. Many of the habitats which we value highly occur only as a result of man's continual management for a specific commodity, for example, reed beds for thatch, or woodland for timber. If, for some reason, management ceases, the habitat will change. Other habitats may be further altered as an indirect result of man's activities. For example the introduction of the rabbit and its subsequent rapid increase in numbers, gave us, amongst others, the short-cropped, herb rich turf which we associate with Downland and Breck. Many of these habitats have been managed in a traditional manner for centuries and animal and plant communities have adapted to them.

Unfortunately, over the last century, many of these old management practices have declined. Coppicing of woodland is no longer practised except on nature reserves as there is now little demand for wattle hurdles as a building material, or for wood as a fuel. Reed beds became overgrown as the demand for thatch fell and peat cuttings have infilled again as more efficient fuels became readily available. Myxomatosis, too, has caused dramatic changes to many grassland areas which, in the absence of rabbit grazing, have become overgrown by scrub.

Many plants and animals associated with these areas have become noticeably scarcer in the last century. It has become obvious that just putting a fence around an area and declaring it a reserve offers insufficient protection to many plants and animals, which although still present, may be declining in numbers.

The early detection of these declines and the identification of the reasons behind them has led to the realisation of a need for research on the requirements of many of our rare species of plants, birds and butterflies. In order to understand the factors limiting the numbers of a particular species, in its natural habitat, detailed studies of the population dynamics must be undertaken. This sort of study enables us to assess the possibilities of manipulating the environment, in order to increase the numbers of the butterfly we are trying to conserve.

Valuable information may be gained, by studying a butterfly in a habitat where it still flourishes and comparing its performance there, with sites where it is declining or from which it has become extinct. In the case of local extinctions, small re-introductions may be necessary to give the required information. If, from these comparisons, it becomes apparent that habitat changes are responsible for the species decline, or extinction, then it may be possible to reverse these changes with a suitable management programme and re-create a habitat in which the butterfly will thrive.

The question of re-introductions is a controversial one, but, as reserves and other suitable habitats become more and more isolated from each other by urban and agricultural land, natural re-colonisation becomes more difficult, particularly for the less mobile species. Thus, the re-introduction of native species to habitats which have been improved for them, by a management programme, may have to be accepted in the future if we are to conserve unique collections of plants and animals intact, in a sufficient number of sites to ensure their survival. The ability to recognise species in need of attention is essential to their successful conservation.

The Biological Records Centre

Mapping schemes give us valuable information on butterfly distributions in the past and at present.

First started in 1954, by the Botanical Society of the British Isles, to map the distribution of plants, the Biological Records Centre (BRC) was originally based in the Botanic Gardens at Cambridge. In 1964, the machinery, records and staff, were moved to the then newly-opened Experimental Station at Monks Wood. In 1967, a new line of research started when, after requests in Entomological and Natural History periodicals, and on radio, some 600 amateur entomologists volunteered to record the butterflies and moths of the British Isles. Today, there are over 2,600 recorders in the country sending in records of Macrolepidoptera to the BRC. In addition, the BRC is also involved in the mapping of many other insect groups as well as reptiles, amphibia and mammals.

The mapping scheme is based on the presence of adult individuals seen in a 10km square. Recorders are asked to survey as many different habitats as possible over a period of years, in order to try and cover the flight periods of species likely to be there. They enter their records on one of three different types of card (see Figure 1). The first (1a) is a card having a list of species on it which may be crossed off when seen. There is room on the card for date, grid reference and habitat notes. More specialised cards exist for the recording of rare species (1b.), or species new to the area ("individual record" cards), and for recording the occurrence of one particular species at several different sites (1c.) (a "one species" card). Recorders are also requested to separate data collected on nature reserves from data for the rest of the 10km square.

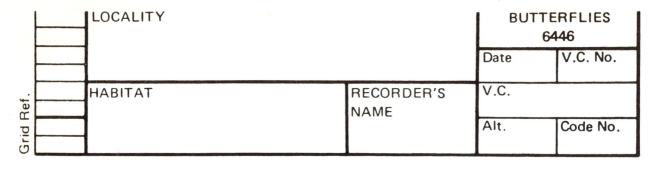

Grid Ref.	LOCALITY		BUTTERFLIES 6446	
			Date	V.C. No.
	HABITAT	RECORDER'S NAME	V.C.	
			Alt.	Code No.

2	Aglais urticae	64	Limenitis camilla
4	Anthocharis cardamines	66	Lycaena dispar
6	Apatura iris	68	Lycaena phlaeas
8	Aphantopus hyperantus	70	Lysandra bellargus
10	Aporia crataegi	71	Lysandra coridon
12	Argynnis aglaia	73	Maculinea arion
13	Argynnis cydippe	75	Maniola jurtina
14	Argynnis euphrosyne	76	Maniola tithonus
15	Argynnis lathonia	78	Melanargia galathea
17	Argynnis paphia	80	Melitaea athalia
18	Argynnis selene	81	Melitaea cinxia
20	Aricia agestis	83	Nymphalis antiopa
21	Aricia allous	84	Nymphalis io
23	Callophrys rubi	85	Nymphalis polychloros
25	Carterocephalus palaemon	88	Ochlodes venata
27	Celastrina argiolus	90	Papilio machaon
29	Coenonympha pamphilus	93	Pararge aegeria
30	Coenonympha tullia	94	Pararge megera
32	Colias australis	98	Pieris brassicae
33	Colias hyale	99	Pieris napi
34	Colias croceus	100	Pieris rapae
36	Cupido minimus	102	Plebejus argus
38	Cyaniris semiargus	104	Polygonia c-album
40	Danaus plexippus	106	Polyommatus icarus
42	Erebia aethiops	108	Pontia daplidice
43	Erebia epiphron	110	Pyrgus malvae
46	Erynnis tages	112	Strymonidia pruni
48	Eumenis semele	113	Strymonidia w-album
50	Euphydryas aurinia	115	Thecla betulae
52	Everes argiades	116	Thecla quercus
54	Gonepteryx rhamni	118	Thymelicus acteon
56	Hamearis lucina	119	Thymelicus lineola
58	Hesperia comma	120	Thymelicus sylvestris
60	Lampides boeticus	122	Vanessa atalanta
62	Leptidea sinapis	123	Vanessa cardui

OTHER SPECIES

Figure 1. (a) BRC butterfly record card

ORDER	Lepidoptera			GENUS & SPECIES	Coenonympha pamphily		SUB-SPECIES
					Small Heath		

COMPILER	M. A. Smith		SOURCE (Collection/Reference)			
			Fld.	Mus.	Lit.	N.C.C. Regional Office (Wilts.)

Grid Reference	V.-C.	Collector/Recorder	Determiner	Locality	Date
31 85 76	7	M. Jones		West Yatton Down	29.5.74
31 84 75	7	B. Smith		Rock Hill	18.5.80
41 33 61	22	M. Hall		Ham Hill	3.8.80
41 33 61	22	T. Bibby		Ham Hill	post 1963

(b) BRC "Individual" record card

ORDER	GENUS & SPECIES		SUB-SPECIES
Lepidoptera	Parange algeria		

VICE-COUNTY	LOCALITY	ALTITUDE m.
Argyll-Main	Letterwalton Bowderlock Argyll	
		ALTITUDE ft.

V.-C. No.	9	8	GRID REFERENCE	1	7	9	1	6	4	0	5	STATUS	NAT	INT	ESC	MIG	CAS	UNK		

RECORDER/COLLECTOR		DATE OF RECORD		COMPILER	
J.Smith		2 0 0 5 1 9 8 0		J. Smith	

DETERMINER	DATE OF DETERMINATION	DATE OF COMPILATION
J. Smith		1 2 0 2 1 9 8 1

STAGE							HOST/FOODPLANT	HABITAT	ASPECT
Ova	Nymph	Skin	♂	♀	Seedling	FL.		Oak/Hazel woodland along small stream	
Larva	Pupa	Skel	♀	Adult	Juv	Veg	Frt		SLOPE

SOURCE	COMMENTS

Biological Records Centre   October 1980   GEN 8

(c) BRC "One species" card

When received by the BRC, the cards are checked and separated into date classes:— pre 1940, 1940-60, 1961-69 and 1970 onwards. The data are then transferred to the Master Card for that particular 10km square and date class. From the Master Card, data are transferred onto Optical Mark Reader (OMR) Computer forms (OPSCAN) and sent to the Science Research Council's Rutherford Computing Laboratory where the information is currently being processed.

The first provisional Atlas of butterflies was published in 1970, examples of which are shown in Figures 2 and 3. A revised edition was issued to recorders in 1975, and it is hoped to produce a definitive atlas of butterflies (for 70 species) in 1981/82 as an ITE publication.

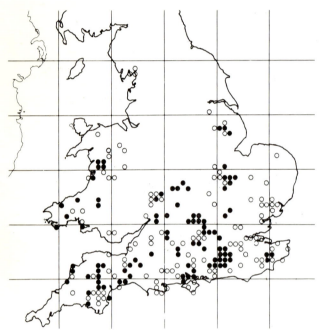

Figure 2. The distribution of the brown hairstreak in England and Wales. ○ pre-1960 ● post 1960.

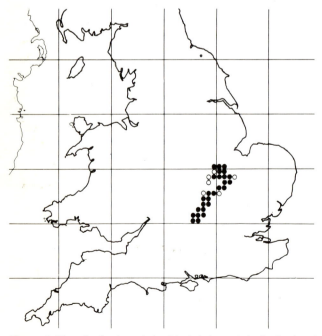

Figure 3. The distribution of the black hairstreak in England and Wales. ○ pre-1960 ● post 1960.

Apart from the value of the mapping scheme itself, the BRC data are invaluable to the ecologist who may be embarking on a detailed study of one species to locate populations for study. From the original cards, it is possible to find the nearest site at which it is possible to carry out a study. Historical data can be abstracted on distribution changes and habitat preferences. Distributions may be correlated with geological, botanical and climatological data and it is also possible to map the decline or expansion of a species in certain areas by mapping date classes separately.

However, the BRC scheme can tell us little about the abundance of butterflies recorded at a particular locality, and, as the decline to extinction of a butterfly may be a very rapid process (as with the chequered skipper *Carterocephalus palaemon* (Plate 2) in the East Midlands), some other method is needed to monitor the abundance of butterflies on a national scale.

The Butterfly Monitoring Scheme

This scheme was started in 1973 by several staff at Monks Wood. The method used was to walk a fixed route (the transect) through Monks Wood, simply counting the numbers of butterflies they saw within limits either side and in front of the recorder. It was found that the results were remarkably consistent, irrespective of the different recorders and despite fluctuations in weather conditions above certain minima of temperature and sunshine.

In 1974, the scheme was expanded to include five other local sites; four reserves and a farm. Two years' results from Monks Wood and one year's from the other five sites were sufficient to convince the Nature Conservancy Council (NCC) that this was a valuable technique suitable for use on nature reserves, to monitor the annual fluctuations in butterfly numbers. Consequently, the NCC commissioned the ITE to expand the scheme to cover as many sites and as great a variety of habitats as possible. Some agricultural and urban sites were included for comparison with the more protected reserve areas. In 1976, there were 38 sites; today, there are over ninety contributors to the scheme (Figure 4).

Essentially, a transect is a fixed route though an area divided into sections according to varying habitat and/or management treatments. The route, once established, must remain unchanged from year to year and should be walked at least once a week between 1st April and 30th September, when weather conditions are suitable. The limits on weather are:—

A transect should not be walked at temperatures below 13°C.

At temperatures between 13-17°C, there must be at least 60% sunshine.

Above 17°C, the amount of sunshine is not critical.

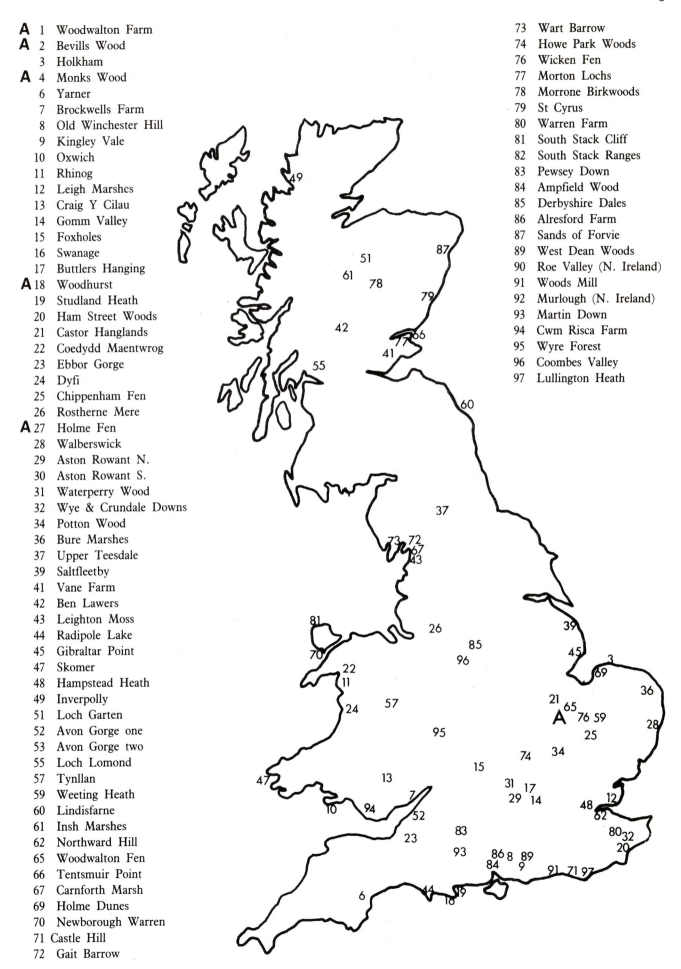

A 1   Woodwalton Farm
A 2   Bevills Wood
3   Holkham
A 4   Monks Wood
6   Yarner
7   Brockwells Farm
8   Old Winchester Hill
9   Kingley Vale
10   Oxwich
11   Rhinog
12   Leigh Marshes
13   Craig Y Cilau
14   Gomm Valley
15   Foxholes
16   Swanage
17   Buttlers Hanging
A 18   Woodhurst
19   Studland Heath
20   Ham Street Woods
21   Castor Hanglands
22   Coedydd Maentwrog
23   Ebbor Gorge
24   Dyfi
25   Chippenham Fen
26   Rostherne Mere
A 27   Holme Fen
28   Walberswick
29   Aston Rowant N.
30   Aston Rowant S.
31   Waterperry Wood
32   Wye & Crundale Downs
34   Potton Wood
36   Bure Marshes
37   Upper Teesdale
39   Saltfleetby
41   Vane Farm
42   Ben Lawers
43   Leighton Moss
44   Radipole Lake
45   Gibraltar Point
47   Skomer
48   Hampstead Heath
49   Inverpolly
51   Loch Garten
52   Avon Gorge one
53   Avon Gorge two
55   Loch Lomond
57   Tynllan
59   Weeting Heath
60   Lindisfarne
61   Insh Marshes
62   Northward Hill
65   Woodwalton Fen
66   Tentsmuir Point
67   Carnforth Marsh
69   Holme Dunes
70   Newborough Warren
71   Castle Hill
72   Gait Barrow

73   Wart Barrow
74   Howe Park Woods
76   Wicken Fen
77   Morton Lochs
78   Morrone Birkwoods
79   St Cyrus
80   Warren Farm
81   South Stack Cliff
82   South Stack Ranges
83   Pewsey Down
84   Ampfield Wood
85   Derbyshire Dales
86   Alresford Farm
87   Sands of Forvie
89   West Dean Woods
90   Roe Valley (N. Ireland)
91   Woods Mill
92   Murlough (N. Ireland)
93   Martin Down
94   Cwm Risca Farm
95   Wyre Forest
96   Coombes Valley
97   Lullington Heath

Figure 4. A map of Britain showing monitoring sites.

Photograph: J. Heath.

Plate 2. Chequered skipper butterfly.

Photograph M. S. Warren.

Plate 4. Adonis blue butterfly.

Photograph: J. Heath.

Plate 1. Small white butterfly.

Photograph: E. Pollard.

Plate 3. Peacock butterfly.

Photograph: J. A. Thomas.

Plate 6. Marsh fritillary butterfly.

Photograph: M. S. Warren.

Plate 8. Lulworth skipper butterfly.

Photograph: M. S. Warren.

Plate 5. Small blue butterfly.

Photograph: M. S. Warren.

Plate 7. Silver-spotted skipper butterfly.

Printed forms are supplied to each recorder (Figure 5), on which he puts the numbers of each species of butterfly seen in each section, together with records of temperature, % sun, windspeed and time of day. From this information, an index of abundance (the sum of the weekly counts) for each species, can be calculated at the end of the year.

Methods of recording and setting up a transect are described in a printed booklet which is sent to each recorder. At the end of each season, the recorders return their completed forms to Monks Wood and the data are punched and fed into the computer. A report on interesting aspects of the year's findings is produced annually. Each recorder, and the appropriate regional officer of the NCC, receives a copy, enabling them to see their results in relation to those from the rest of the country.

At Monks Wood, where the scheme has been running for 6 years, it has been possible to relate the distributions of butterflies in the wood, to management differences, foodplant location, nectar sources (Table 1) and shelter. Similar comparisons will soon be possible for many other sites, and, in addition, valuable data on the flight periods of butterflies are being acquired. Although monitoring does not itself provide answers to the reasons for fluctuations in butterfly numbers, it does provide much background information for more detailed research and suggests topics which might profitably be investigated.

It is hoped that the scheme will give early warning of species which are becoming endangered. If, for example, a species in one reserve is declining more than elsewhere, it may be possible to compare the reserve with other, better sites and suggest a management programme to improve the hatitat for that species.

However, this scheme also has its limitations. It cannot tell us anything about the size of the population we are sampling. The index of abundance is not a population estimate. It is not possible to compare the numbers of small skippers in Monks Wood for example with the numbers at Woodwalton Farm and say one site is "better" than the other. We simply count the number of adult butterflies seen. We do not know whether they are breeding in the area, feeding, or simply passing through. For this reason, in the summer of 1978, an attempt was made to develop the transect technique to see if it was possible, using very simple methods, to get reasonably accurate estimates of a population's size in small discrete areas.

For this study, five species of butterfly, which are fairly local in their distribution, were chosen :—The adonis blue, (Plate 4), small blue (Plate 5), marsh fritillary (Plate 6), silver-spotted skipper (Plate 7) and Lulworth skipper (Plate 8). Several colonies of each species were located and the habitats of each individual species were compared, notes being made of habitat size, different management regimes and colony history. Having done this for each site, a transect was set up $1\frac{1}{2}$ m wide to cover the whole of the area in which the butterfly was known to occur. A count was then made and an index value obtained for the species being studied. This index was then divided by the total length of the transect and the numbers per square metre calculated. By multiplying this figure by the total area of the site it was possible to obtain a "population" index for each site, for each of the five species. Having done this, the sites were then re-surveyed, this time using mark and recapture techniques to estimate the total population size. The two figures were then compared and very close agreement was found. Rather few sites have been compared for each species, so far, though several days' work has been done on most sites. There is a highly significant statistical agreement between the two types of population estimate.

This new method of estimating population size is much quicker and easier to do than mark and recapture methods and it enables us to compare the relative sizes of populations of butterflies of the same species at different sites. It promises to be a very useful method in the future for surveys which are done within a limited budget and time.

Table 1. Shows the index of abundance of peacocks *Inachis io* (L.) (Plate 3) and the number of teasels (*Dipsacus fullonum*) flowering, per section of the transect.

Section number	Number teasels flowering	Index of abundance of peacocks (autumn brood)
1	225	21·7
2	14	1·3
3	0	0
4	0	0
5	42	9·0
6	24	0·7
7	68	2·7
8	622	39·2
9	1113	62·2
10	860	63·4
11	5	9·0
12	0	1·0
13	49	10·7
14	1	0

BUTTERFLY CENSUS

YEAR 1-2	80	DATE 3-5	18-8	RECORDER 6-8	T.J.B.		
9-11		SITE NAME 12-17	MONKS WOOD			18-19	
START TIME 20-23	10.55	END TEMP. °C 24-26	20	% SUN 27-28	85	END WIND SPEED 29	3

	30-32	33-35	36	39	42	45	48	51	54	57	60	63	66	69	72	75	78-80
SECTION		1	2	3	4	5	6	7	8	9	10	11	12	13	14	15	TOTAL
BRIMSTONE	54		2♂♂					2♀		3♂♂♀		3♂♂♂		1♀			11
COMMON BLUE	106																
GREEN-VEINED WHITE	99	15	6	5	1	19		9	5	4	6	14	3	9			96
HEDGE BROWN	76	7				4	6	2	10	1	6	2		1			39
LARGE SKIPPER	88																
LARGE WHITE	98								2		1			1			4
MEADOW BROWN	75	4	2			6	21		17	8	3	4		7			72
ORANGE TIP	4																
PEACOCK	84	1	3			8			1	1	2	5		19			40
RED ADMIRAL	122																
RINGLET	8																
SMALL COPPER	68																
SMALL HEATH	29																
SMALL SKIPPER	120																
SMALL TORTOISESHELL	2																
SMALL WHITE	100	2	1			1					1	3		2			10
WALL	94						1		2								3
SPECKLED WOOD								2									2
HOLY BLUE														1			1
SECTION		1	2	3	4	5	6	7	8	9	10	11	12	13	14	15	
SUNSHINE																	

NOTES: PLEASE TOTAL EACH SQUARE

Figure 5. Form supplied to recorders in the Butterfly Monitoring Scheme for use during weekly counts.

14

The Porton Down Survey

This survey was started in 1973. Porton Down is owned by the Ministry of Defence and is the largest remaining area of chalk grassland in southern England. The area has had little or no management for the past 20-30 years and has an abundance of butterflies, 36 species in all, many of which although not rare, are local in their distribution, e.g. the chalkhill blue *Lysandra coridon* (Plate 9) and the dark green fritillary *Argynnis aglaia* (Plate 10).

The study was directed at understanding the impact that the cessation of agricultural management had had on the Porton Ranges, and at examining the possible link between this lack of management and the abundance of butterflies. There were many problems associated with sampling the area, as the MOD often shut down large sections of the Ranges at short notice. Hence, many of the methods of sampling which require repeated visits to the same area, e.g. the transect method could not be used. It was decided to survey the area by

dividing it into 93 $\frac{1}{2} \times \frac{1}{2}$ km squares and recording the presence of each of the different species of butterflies in each square (Figure 6). A distribution map for each species has been produced and it is hoped to follow up this initial survey with a study of the distribution of food plants and nectar sources for some of the species.

However, only a much more detailed population study can tell us what is governing the numbers of butterflies and what that population requires in order to survive. Six of these detailed studies have been completed, or are in progress, mainly on species which are either rare or have undergone dramatic changes in their distribution over recent years.

Many of our rarer species have extremely demanding habitat requirements, so that minor changes in their habitat management can cause rapid changes in their numbers. Often, these habitat changes are almost indiscernable as they are happening so slowly. Therefore, long term population studies are needed to enable

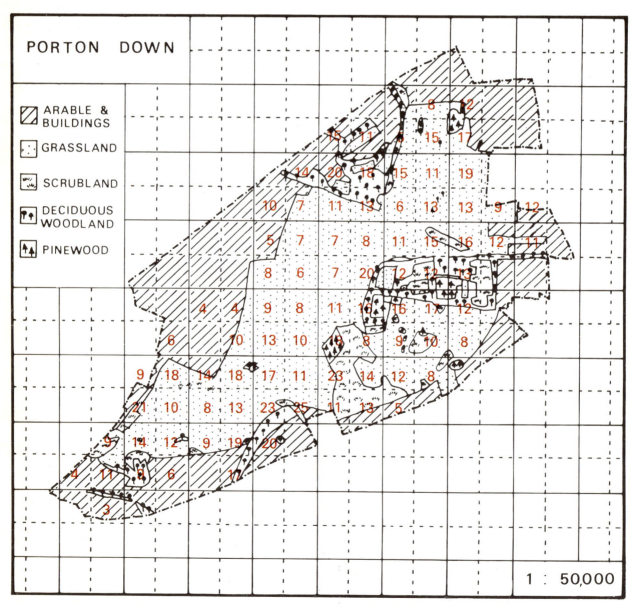

Figure 6. The distribution of the number of species of butterfly present in each ½ x ½ km sq related to the various habitats at Porton.

us to understand a butterfly's requirements and to suggest an appropriate management regime for its successful conservation.

The black hairstreak
(Strymonidia pruni)

The black hairstreak (Plate 11) is one of our rarest woodland butterflies. It lays its eggs on blackthorn *Prunus spinosa*. Despite the wide distribution of the food plant, the black hairstreak's distribution is limited to what is left of the East Midlands' forest belt on the low lying clays which run from Oxford to Peterborough (Fig. 3).

Because of the physical difficulties involved in working on an animal which is not only scarce but usually lays eggs high up on mature blackthorn scrub, the study was aimed at comparing past and present sites and distributions of the species in Britain. Detailed comparative studies of the habitats in which the butterfly occurs in good numbers, and those from where it has become extinct, were undertaken in order to try to understand what limits the distribution and abundance of the species. Simultaneously, a study was made to obtain population data from the hairstreak colony in Monks Wood and information on the factors affecting the survival of the larval stages of the butterfly (Table 2).

of blackthorn around glades, or along rides, within a woodland system (Figure 7).

The black hairstreak is very slow to colonise new areas. Small discrete populations may remain in a limited area for many years. Its inability to re-colonise new areas has lead to its extinction on many sites where part of a wood has been clear-felled, even though there is other suitable habitat nearby. Its present distribution is limited to the East Midlands forest belt which is a region where woodland has been traditionally managed on an unusually long (more than 20 years) coppice cycle. Elsewhere in the country, coppice cycles were usually much shorter, making it impossible for the butterfly to keep pace with its rapidly changing environment. All recent extinctions are directly attributable to modern forestry and agricultural practices, i.e. clear-felling prior to replacing with conifers or conversion to farmland.

As a result of these findings, management recomendations have been made for the conservation of this insect. No more than 25% of a site should be cleared at any one time and the blackthorn should be managed on a 20-30 year cycle. In areas of dense scrub, a series of glades and rides should be cut to give the effect shown in Figure 7. Ideally cutting of blackthorn should be done in June, at a time when the insect is in its pupal stage. Adults emerging later will then be able to search out new areas of live blackthorn nearby.

Table 2. The percentage survival of black hairstreaks in Monks Wood in 1971 and 1972 combined. (the number of individuals from which the percentage survival of each stage was obtained is given in brackets after each stage).

Stage	Number (%)	Mortality in each stage (%)	Cause of mortality
Egg (74)	100	36	Parasites (19%) Failure to hatch (11%) Invertebrate predation (5%) Empty egg = sterile? (1%)
1st instar larva (84)	64	47	Invertebrate predation
2nd instar larva (44)	34	32	Mainly invertebrate predation
3rd instar larva (30)	23	48	Mainly bird predation
4th instar larva (16)	12	48	Mainly bird predation
Pupa (9)	5	80	Mainly bird predation Small % parasites
Adult	1·1		

Initially, each site was compared with those at Monks Wood and Bernwood Forest. These populations had been known and visited for over twenty years and there was considerable information available as to their size and fluctuations. The study suggested that the black hairstreak will breed on blackthorn which is not more than 75% shaded by the woodland canopy. It will also lay on mature, overgrown hedges, close too and sheltered by woodland. However, the preferred habitat of the butterfly is a network of sheltered sunny banks

Because of its inability to re-colonise cleared areas, small, local, re-introductions of this species may be necessary, where an old cleared site becomes suitable once more for the butterfly. The present-day population in Monks Wood was a re-introduction after the wood had been clear felled in 1918. If these recommendations are followed, the black hairstreak is capable of reaching high densities in quite small areas, as it has in areas of Monks Wood where these proposals have been implemented.

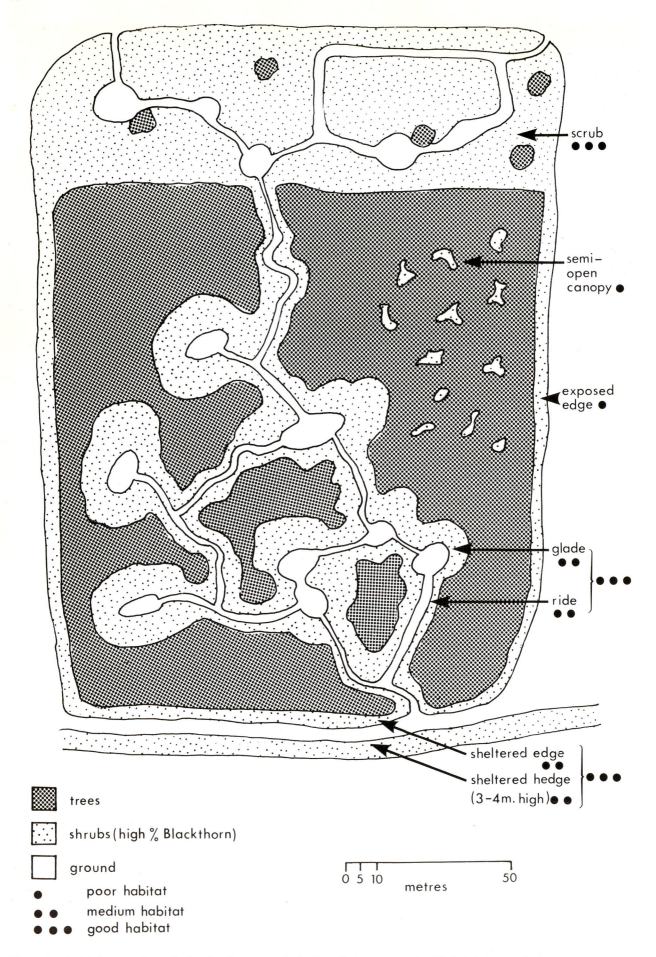

scrub ●●●

semi-
open
canopy ●

exposed
edge ●

glade ●●

ride ●●

sheltered edge ●●

sheltered hedge
(3-4m. high) ●●

●●● (good habitat bracket)

trees

shrubs (high % Blackthorn)

ground

●   poor habitat
●●   medium habitat
●●●   good habitat

0 5 10   50
          metres

Figure 7. Aerial diagram of wood, showing the range of situations that can support a black hairstreak colony.

The brown hairstreak
(Thecla betulae)

A colony of the brown hairstreak (Plate 12) has been intensively studied at Crowleigh in Surrey for 7 years and detailed life tables have been compiled for this species. The information gained from this study has enabled us to understand many of the factors governing the distribution and abundance of this species in Britain. The brown hairstreak is at the northern edge of its range in this country. Though widely distributed throughout southern Britain, it is a very local species which is rarely found in large numbers (Figure 2). It lays its eggs at low densities over large areas, usually very close to the ground on young blackthorn. Wood edges and hedges within 2 km of a wood are equally favoured by egg-laying females, which will even lay on closely cropped, intensively managed hedges.

beetles and spiders. Birds become the most important predators in the third and fourth instars. The main predators of the pupae are small mammals, such as the wood mouse and field mouse, and a high, but variable, proportion of the pupae is taken each year by these animals. By the time the pupal stage is reached, up to 90% of the eggs and larvae may have been taken by arthropod or avian predators. Therefore, the survival of the pupae is a very important factor in determining the number of adults which will emerge in the next generation.

The temperature at the time of larval and pupal development greatly affects the amount of time spent in these stages (Tables 3 and 4). As mortalities are extremely high at this time, the more quickly a larva can pass through its development, the better its chance of survival.

Table 3. Larval development time at Cranleigh

Year	Mean larval time (days)	Mean temp. °C.	Difference from mean 1930-60
1970	$42 \cdot 6 \pm 0 \cdot 23$	May 12·9 June 16·5	+1·7 +1·7
1971	$51 \cdot 5 \pm 0 \cdot 38$	May 11·7 June 13·1	0·0 −1·7
1972	$62 \cdot 0 \pm 1 \cdot 35$	May 10·5 June 11·7	−1·2 −3·1

Prior to breeding, the adults tend to aggregate around a large tree, or group of trees, in a wood. There they pair and feed on honeydew produced by aphids feeding on the leaves of the trees. After pairing, the females disperse to lay their eggs. If high densities of adults aggregate at the start of the season, there is evidence to suggest that many adults disperse without laying their eggs in the immediate vicinity.

The number of eggs laid in the previous year is the most important single factor influencing adult numbers. This number is dependent upon emigration, longevity and the weather (adults are inactive a temperature below c.19 °C).

The conservation management of the brown hairstreak is in many ways far more difficult than that of the black

Table 4. Pupal development at Cranleigh

Year	Pupal time (days)	Mean air temp. (July) °C	Deviation from 1930-60 mean
1970	38·1	15·9	−0·9
1971	29·4	17·1	+0·3
1972	35·0	16·1	−0·7

Many eggs are lost during the winter months as a result of hedge cutting. Samples taken from the hedges showed that on average, in one 10 km square, 45% of the eggs were lost due to hedge management during the winter months. As there is a tendency for the brown hairstreak to lay on new growth, the eggs are very susceptible to loss when the hedge is trimmed.

The eggs hatch in the spring and the young larvae feed on the blackthorn leaves. In the early stages, many larvae are taken by invertebrate predators, such as

hairstreak. Fortunately, at present, it is not in immediate need of protection. However, although it may be, possible to protect the woods in which the adults pair it is extremely difficult to preserve the hedges around the wood, in which the butterfly breeds. The extensive destruction of hedgerows in East Anglia has probably been responsible for the reduction in the numbers of brown hairstreaks in this area, many local populations, including the one at Monks Wood, having become extinct.

18

Photograph: J. A. Thomas.

Plate 10.   Dark green fritillary butterfly.

Photograph: M. S. Warren.

Plate 12.   Brown hairstreak butterfly.

Photograph: M. S. Warren.

Plate 9.   Chalkhill blue butterfly.

Photograph: M. S. Warren.

Plate 11.   Black hairstreak butterfly.

Plate 14. White admiral butterfly, hibernaculum.
Photograph: E. Pollard.

Plate 16. Wicken Fen, Cambridgeshire.
Photograph: Marney Hall

Photograph: M. S. Warren.

Plate 13. White admiral butterfly.

Photograph: Marney Hall.

Plate 15. Swallowtail butterfly.

The white admiral
(Ladoga camilla) (Plate 13)

This butterfly expanded its range in the 1940's (Figure 8). The reasons for this expansion and the population ecology of the species in Monks Wood NNR have been studied in detail, from 1972-1978 (Pollard 1979). By studying the species in detail and constructing life tables from the six years' data obtained, it was possible to interpret the factors governing the annual fluctuations

larva will eat the leaf it has chosen straight across ar right angles to the mid-rib (Plate 14) and spin the two edges of this small triangle of leaf together. The petiole is also attached to the main stem, using silk, to prevent the leaf falling off in the autumn (Figure 10). The larva stays in the hibernaculum until the following April. As the temperature rises, it emerges to start feeding again, moulting twice more before pupating on the underside of a honeysuckle leaf. The adult emerges from the pupa about 3 weeks later.

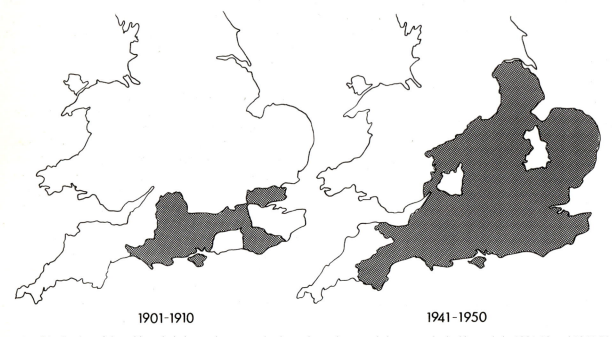

1901-1910

1941-1950

Figure 8. Distribution of the white admiral on a vice-county basis as shown by records in entomological journals in 1901-10 and 1941-50 to show the change in range during the period.

in the population at Monks Wood. Like the brown hairstreak, the white admiral is near the northern edge of its range in Britain. The adult butterflies are on the wing in July. The males take up position around prominent trees in the wood and intercept passing females. If the females are newly emerged they will mate, but, if they have already paired, they will usually reject the male and carry on searching for suitable egg-laying

Many larvae are lost during the early instars to invertebrate predators, but the most important factor, governing the year to year fluctuation in population size, is the survival of late larval and pupal stages. Up to 80% of the larvae entering the fifth instar may be lost, it is thought mainly due to bird predation.

Figure 9. Typical leaf damage caused by the early larval instars of the white admiral to honeysuckle leaves.

sites, or food. The females lay their eggs, on long mature strands of honeysuckle (Lonicera periclymenum) which hang down from the trees in lightly shaded areas within the wood, at ride edges, or around the edges of glades (Figure 9). When the larvae are in their third instar, they start to construct a hibernaculum, or refuge, in which they will pass the winter. Each

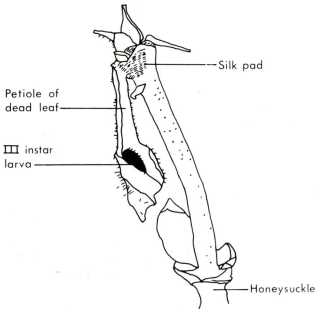

Figure 10. The hibernaculum of the white admiral.

As with the brown hairstreak, there is a very strong correlation between the temperature and the speed of larval development. Moreover there is a very strong correlation between earliness of season and survival to the adult stage. The temperature in June is particularly important, as it is at this time that the large larvae and pupae are most vulnerable to predation. The more quickly they pass through these stages, the more adults emerge in July (Figure 11).

As a result of these findings, the meteorological data for the South and Central England in 1900-1977 were examined. The spread of the white admiral had been

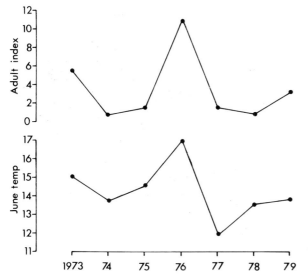

Figure 11. Adult index of abundance, based on transect counts and June temperatures.

well documented in entomological journals, as, until the 1940's it had been a relatively scarce insect. Therefore, its occurrence at a new site, or its presence at sites in large numbers, was often commented upon. Figure 12 shows that the spread of the white admiral in the 1930's was associated with a period of very warm summers (particularly Junes).

Another factor associated with the spread of the butterfly has been the increase in habitat suitable for the butterfly. Open coppice is not a suitable habitat for honeysuckle. Also honeysuckle is regarded by woodsmen and foresters as a weed which damages the timber crop, and it is very strictly controlled in commercially managed woodlands. However, the decline of commercial coppicing, since the turn of the century has meant that many woods have become neglected and honeysuckle has become more abundant as coppices have become overgrown. Thus, the warm summers of the 1930's caused an abundance of adult butterflies, and these were able to disperse to new areas which were becoming more suitable for colonisation by the butterfly.

The white admiral arrived at Monks Wood in the early 1940's. Around the same time, it also colonized several other local woods. Despite many cool summers since, it has remained in Monks Wood, though it has subsequently disappeared from the other woods nearby. Some of these woods have been cleared and planted with conifers, though others have continued as neglected coppice. Although larger than the rest, the main difference between Monks Wood and these other woodlands seems to be the ride management. The rides in Monks Wood are wide and sunny, and provide many vantage points at which males can aggregate. The rides also produce areas of light shade at their edges which seem to be the preferred sites for egg-laying females. The conservation of this species therefore seems dependent on maintaining a series of rides and glades within neglected coppice or lightly shaded woodland in which the butterfly can breed.

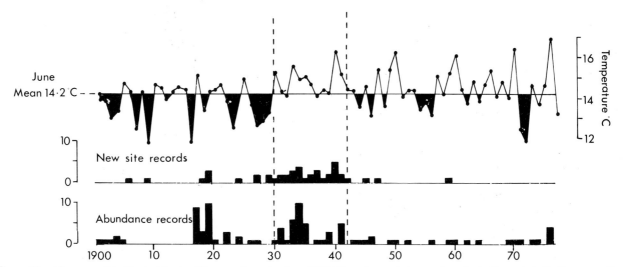

Figure 12. Mean monthly 'Central England' temperatures for June 1900-77, and records from entomological journals indicating spread to a new area and unusual abundance.

The swallowtail butterfly
(Papilio machaon)

Once found throughout the East Anglian fens, the swallowtail (Plate 15) is now confined to marshes around the Norfolk Broads. Until the early 1950's a small, isolated colony of swallowtails survived at Wicken Fen (Plate 16) in Cambridgeshire, but after its extinction there, repeated attempts to re-introduce the butterfly failed.

In 1970, a study was started aimed at understanding the requirements of the butterfly in its present habitats, and also at finding out the reasons for its extinction at Wicken Fen (Dempster, King & Lakhani 1976). The study examined four main topics. First, a detailed study was made of the population ecology of the swallowtail in the Norfolk Broads. Second, a comparative study was made of a small population of swallowtails, introduced as eggs to Wicken Fen. Third, a comparative study was made of the performance of the food plant, milk parsley *Peucedanum palustre*, in Norfolk and at Wicken. Finally, a morphometric study was made of the shape and size of swallowtails in museum collections to see if any detectable genetic differences had evolved between the two populations (Norfolk and Wicken) which could preclude the successful establishment at Wicken of a population reared from Norfolk stock.

The results showed that the survival of the larval stages at Wicken was very similar to that in Norfolk. (Figure 13). Nor were there any detectable differences in size and shape between present day Norfolk swallowtails and those from Wicken. However, large differences were found between the plants at Wicken and those from the Broads. Norfolk plants live longer, grow taller and produce more seed than those from Wicken. However, this difference was not due to genetic differences between the plants from Norfolk and Wicken as they performed equally well, under glass house conditions.

As peat shrinks and oxidises when fen land is drained, Wicken has become an island of high ground surrounded by the much lower agricultural land of the Cambridgeshire fens. For this reason, the fen has gradually been drying out, despite efforts to keep the water table high by the construction of clay banks and dykes. Up to forty years ago, the fen would have flooded every spring, as are the broads today, but spring flooding is now rare. The seed of milk parsley is almost certainly dispersed by water, and the spring floods, as well as dispersing the seed, produce an early flush of growth from the established plants. This growth helps the plant to "get away" earlier so that by the beginning of June, when the adult butterflies are on the wing, the new growth of the plant is above the level of the surr-

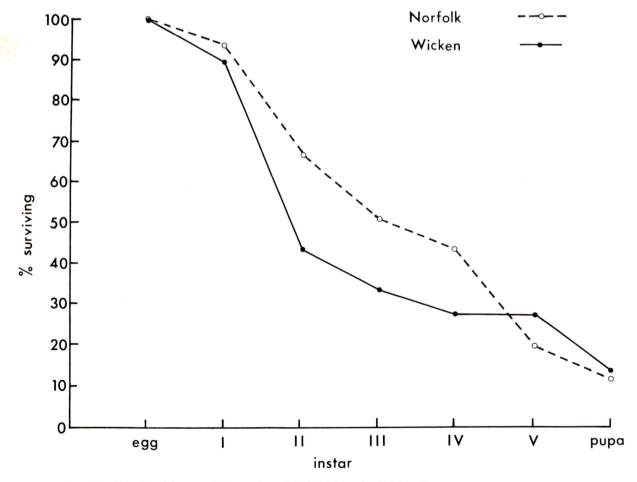

Figure 13. Survival of the larval instars of the swallowtail in Norfolk and at Wicken Fen.

ounding sedge. Females will lay only on those parts of the plant which are exposed above the surrounding vegetation. If insufficient plants are in the right stage of growth, few eggs will be laid, and those which are laid, will tend to be clumped on the more suitable plants. A programme of clearance was started in the 1960's, aimed at opening up more of the fen and linking together existing cleared areas. During the autumn and winter of 1974-75, several thousand milk parsley plants were put into these newly-cleared areas and around the mere on the adjoining Adventurers' Fen. The spring of 1975 was exceptionally wet, and spring floods at Wicken (the first for several years) persisted until the middle of May. These conditions caused the milk parsley plants to do exceptionally well and it was decided to release the swallowtails, which had been reared for this purpose from eggs collected in Norfolk three years previously. Male and female swallowtails were introduced to the fen throughout the month of June and their progress was monitored by counting the number of eggs laid in five fixed transects, 25 m × 1 m, in different parts of the fen.

The drought of 1976 severely affected the performance of the milk parsley and the high temperatures and low humidity badly affected the adults that emerged that year. Many more adults emerged in 1976 than had been previously introduced, but the drought, followed by exceptionally poor weather in two successive Junes, has affected egg laying and severly reduced the number of swallowtails on the fen, and the population has now died out again (Table 5).

In Norfolk, many of the Broads where the swallowtail used to breed have now become overgrown by scrub and are no longer suitable for the butterfly. However, those areas of the broads where the swallowtail still persists e.g. Hickling and the Bure Marshes, are probably adequate to ensure the survival of this, our largest, butterfly. Conservation measures are needed to ensure that the insect's habitat is managed in such a way that the milk parsley will flourish. Scrub encroachment, on the one hand, and the erosion of the reed margins of the broads on the other, both destroy the relatively narrow strip of land in which *Peucedanum* grows and the swallowtail breeds. Extensive management of the Bure

Table 5. Number of eggs laid in the fixed transect at Wicken Fen

Year	No. 25 m transects	No. eggs in transects
1975	4	270
1976	4	65
1977	5	26
1978	5	27
1979	5	0

Marshes has greatly improved this area for the swallowtail and a flourishing population exists there now, where there were relatively few before the management programme was started in the 1970's.

The management of Wicken Fen, for the swallowtail, has proved far more difficult. The relative dryness of the fen continues to be a problem. Scrub encroachment in these conditions is rapid and fields must be cut every three years to prevent them from becoming covered by bushes. The construction of a series of sluices and dykes to keep the water table at a constant level, and from which the fen could be flooded every winter, is prohibitively expensive, and it seems unlikely that such an ambitious project will be undertaken in the immediate future. Thus, the future of the swallowtail at Wicken, and indeed of the fen itself in the long term, remains precarious. Without a determined attempt to create the wet conditions essential to the survival of both the insect and its habitat, both are destined to be lost.

The large blue
(Maculinae arion)

The large blue (Plate 17) is the rarest British butterfly and is a member of the *Lycaenidae*. It was once found much more extensively throughout southern Britain, associated with open heaths and downs where thyme, its food plant, flourishes. Since the turn of the century the large blue has disappeared from many of the areas where it was previously found in Northamptonshire, the Cotswolds and Somerset, but, during the 1950's, the decline accelerated, until by 1973 there was only one site left, in the West County.

Many Lycaenids are associated at some stage of their development with ants. The large blue's survival depends on its being adopted for part of its life cycle by ants, in this case from the genus *Myrmica*. The adult butterfly is on the wing at the end of June and in early July. Females lay their eggs amongst the flower buds of thyme and, on hatching, the larva moves to the older florets where it feeds on the newly developing seeds. After the second moult, the larva will leave the plant on which it is feeding and drop to the ground close by. There, it starts to exude a sticky sweet substance from the posterior gland and this secretion attracts the ants to the larva. An ant will start to "milk" the larva for this secretion (Plate 18) and after several hours will carry the larva down into its nest. There, the larva will spend the winter, feeding on the ant grubs, and it is in the ant's nest that the larva will complete its development. After pupating, the butterfly will emerge from the ants' nest the following June.

Many causes were suggested to be responsible for the decline of the large blue ; climatic change, over-collecting, genetic deterioration due to inbreeding, not enough thyme, habitat destruction, to name but a few. In 1972, a detailed study was started on the species and four sites in the west country were examined. From two of these sites, the large blue had recently become extinct. These two sites had many features in common. Thyme was abundant there, and the sites were ungrazed, but very few *Myrmica* ants were to be found. The third site had held a very large colony of large blues

Plate 17. Large blue butterfly.
Photograph: J. A. Thomas.

Plate 18. Ant 'milking' large blue butterfly larva.
Photograph: J. A. Thomas.

Photograph: M. S. Warren. Plate 20. Silverwashed fritillary butterfly.

Photograph: J. A. Thomas. Plate 22. High brown fritillary butterfly.

Photograph: M. S. Warren. Plate 19. Wood white butterfly and egg after oviposition.

Photograph: M. S. Warren. Plate 21. Pearl-bordered fritillary butterfly.

until the late sixties but this colony had been rapidly diminishing in size. The site was lightly grazed and thyme was abundant, but only 60% of the habitat which was suitable for egg laying was within the territory of a species of *Myrmica*. The fourth site was the smallest of the four, but contained a flourishing population of the butterfly. Of the four sites, it had much the lowest density of thyme, but 100% of the available habitat was within the territory of *Myrmica* ants and the site was being heavily grazed.

Population studies were started at both sites, but the butterfly died out on site 3 in 1974. However, at site 4, the study revealed several very interesting facts. There are four species of *Myrmica* which will support the caterpillars of the large blue in captivity, but, in the wild, only two of these are found in conjunction with thyme; *Myrmica scabrinodis* and *M. sabuleti*. By studying the survival of larvae in the ants' nests on site 4, it was found that the survival of larvae was five times better if they were taken by *M. subuleti* than if they were taken by *M. scabrinodis*. The relative abundance of these two species was found to be associated with different turf heights. Thyme will grow in turf up to 10 cm high, but *M. sabuleti* forages almost exclusively in turf under 2 cm high. If the turf height starts to exceed this level, the numbers of *M. sabuleti* decline rapidly and *M. scabrinodis* becomes more abundant.

Experiments showed that small changes in management produced rapid changes in ant numbers. One experiment involved burning a small area, only 10% of which was foraged by *M. sabuleti*. Three and a half years after burning, followed by grazing, all the ground was being foraged by *M. sabuleti*. As the turf was allowed to grow in control areas, *M. scabrinodis* again became predominant, once more showing a very rapid response to management. With no management at all, *Myrmica* numbers decline rapidly, far more rapidly than does the number of thyme plants. The advent of myxomatosis will most certainly have severely affected many of the old large blue sites as many of them were previously very heavily grazed by rabbits. At the same time, it became uneconomic to graze rough 'unimproved' hillsides intensively, and the reduction in grazing combined with a reduction in rabbit numbers will have quickly affected the height of the turf. Once the turf was allowed to grow, the ants on which the large blue depends for survival will have disappeared.

Finally, the detailed population study carried out at site 4 for six years suggested that the single most important factor governing the annual fluctuations in size of the population, was survival in the ants' nests. It was found that, if more than five larvae were taken into one nest, none would survive. Hence, the carrying capacity of the habitat is governed by the number of ant nests present.

Having discovered the importance of the correct species of ant to the large blue, a survey was carried out on all the sites where the large blue had been recorded. Forty-five of these sites still had an abundance of thyme plants, but on examination of the turf height and ant numbers, it became apparent that the large blue had almost certainly become extinct in these areas as a result of a decrease in ant numbers due to lack of grazing.

From 1974-1979, conservation of the large blue centred around the last remaining site, in the west country. This site is now heavily grazed all year, in order to maintain a short turf in which *M. sabuleti* is abundant. The grazing there has been increased, and adjacent areas have been cleared, planted with thyme and grazed. *M. sabuleti*, in these new areas, has become very abundant.

In 1973, many large blue butterflies emerged at site 4, so many, in fact, that the carrying capacity of the habitat was exceeded and the numbers fell drastically in 1974 because of poor survival in the ants' nests due to overcrowding in the previous winter. The population had not recovered when the adverse weather conditions which have so badly affected the swallowtail at Wicken Fen also affected this, the last colony of the large blue in Britain. The west country suffered a severe drought in 1975, as well as the more general drought in 1976. The two successive poor summers of 1977 and 1978 since then have reduced the population of large blues to a very low level, and it is now known that this last remaining colony has not survived.

The history of this study demonstrates how essential it is to recognise when a species is declining and to initiate a study of the insect before it becomes too scarce to save. The only consolation left to us, is that although the large blue has become extinct in this country, we do at least know why.

The wood white
(Lepitidea sinapis)

The wood white (Plate 19) is a woodland butterfly which was formerly far more widespread in Britain, but its range has been contracting since the turn of the century. Recently, however, the butterfly has shown a marked, though small, expansion. These changes in the distribution and abundance of the butterfly are thought to be associated with changes in woodland management and forestry practice.

Over half of the sites where the wood white occurs in England are in Forestry Commission plantations, where it breeds on several species of vetch. At Yardley Chase, where a study of the ecology of this butterfly is being conducted, the insect shows a preference for meadow vetchling (*Lathyrus pratensis*). The wide, sheltered rides of the F.C. woods apparently provide an ideal habitat for this butterfly. It is a very weak-flying butterfly and like the black hairstreak is a very poor coloniser of new habitats. It is thought that the decline of coppicing and maintenance of wide rides for timber extraction at the turn of the century was responsible for the initial contraction in range of this butterfly. As the rides, glades and coppices became overgrown the breeding areas for this butterfly would have disappeared. However, modern forestry practices have once again provided habitats in which this butterfly can breed successfully. The wide rides provide an ideal habitat for both the butterfly and its foodplants, but the poor colonising ability of the insect has meant that its recovery and expansion of range has been very slow.

Detailed studies of the butterfly's ecology have revealed that the quantity of foodplant may be important to the species' survival, as the females appear to be unable to detect the foodplant visually and can only recognise it by actually coming into physical contact with the plant. A low density of foodplants would almost certainly lead to a reduction in the number of eggs a female would lay, as she would have to spend far more time searching for suitable egg-laying sites. It is hoped to make recommendations for the management of this species when the project is complete in 1980.

The pearl-bordered fritillary
(Argynnis euphrosyne)

The decline of yet another group of woodland butterflies, the fritillaries, particularly from the eastern counties and East Midlands, was responsible for the start of new research in 1978. By using the data from the BRC, and separating them into several different date classes, it was possible to show the extent of the decline of three woodland fritillaries; the silver-washed fritillary (*Argynnis paphia*) (Plate 20), the pearl-bordered fritillary (*Argynnis euphrosyne*) (Plate 21) and the high brown fritillary (*Argynnis cydippe*) (Plate 22) particularly since the 1960's. The high brown fritillary has shown the most marked decline, but its habits make it an extremely difficult subject for an autecological study (Figure 14).

All three species feed on violets and it is thought that, once again, changes in woodland management are responsible for the reduction in numbers of these butterflies. All were present in Monks Wood until the 1950's and the last one to become extinct was the silver-washed fritillary in 1968. None of these butterflies now occurs anywhere in the county, and the nearest study site is Bernwood Forest in Oxfordshire. It is hoped to study a small colony of pearl-bordered fritillaries in some detail in order to try to understand the reasons for their decline.

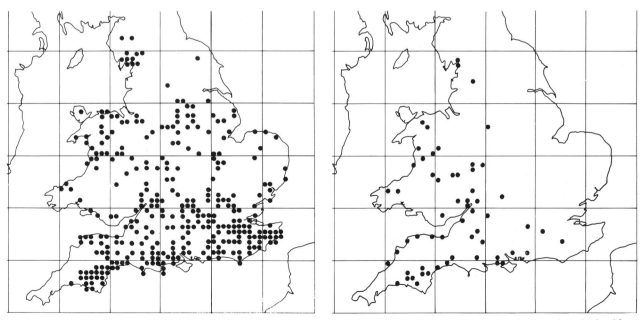

Figure 14. Maps showing the distribution of the high brown fritillary (a) all records 1940-78, (b) post 1970 records, from data obtained from the BRC.

Conclusion

From the studies described in this booklet it is obvious that each species of butterfly has very detailed requirements and habitat preferences. A full understanding of these requirements is essential if we are to ensure that no more species of British butterfly become extinct. Only a detailed autecological study can reveal the exact needs of each species and such studies require several years of painstaking research to be of value. However, it is hoped that, with the range of information available to the Institute, it will be possible to recognise those species in need of conservation and make the appropriate management recommendations to those who are responsible for their preservation.